THE RELAXATION REFLEX

THE RELAXATION REFLEX

Robin Sands

2000

First published in 2001 by Management Books 2000 Ltd
Cowcombe House
Cowcombe Hill
Chalford
Gloucestershire GL6 8HP
Tel. 01285 760 722
Fax. 01285 760 708
E-mail: m.b.2000@virgin.net

Printed and bound in Great Britain by Biddles, Guildford

British Library Cataloguing in Publication Data is available

ISBN 1-85252-370-0

For a complete list of Management Books 2000 titles,
visit our web-site on http://www.mb2000.com

Contents

Introduction

This book is about the **Relaxation Reflex**, a natural phenomenon that occurs spontaneously when the right conditions are present. This reflex is the solution, inherent in all human beings, to what we call stress.

Stress cannot be circumvented, nor can it be overpowered. But it will unwind quite naturally given the right circumstances, and this book explains in detail how to give it the chance to do so.

What happens spontaneously cannot be repeated until an understanding of the cause has been acquired. Similarly, nothing can be changed until an awareness of that thing has been reached. We only seem helpless in the face of stress because we are not conscious of its process.

As a race, we have a strong tendency to blame things "out there" for our internal discomfort. But no matter how clever or powerful we are, we can only control certain portions of our external reality. To this end, many people allay their anxiety and offset their sense of tension by being organised and goal oriented. These are good practices, but in themselves will not yield holistic health, i.e. harmony between mind, body and spirit.

Understanding always reduces fear and increases creative opportunities, and the Relaxation Reflex is certainly no exception to this rule. It will give you the perceptive tools to recognise the source of discomfort in your body. Conditions such as migraine, lower back pain and digestive disorders do not come to us by accident. They are quite definite signs that our internal equilibrium is out of balance. Potions and lotions may be able to dull our awareness of this imbalance but they cannot take it away. A surgeon's knife may be able to remove offending parts of our body, but no matter how sharp the blade, it will not be able to reach the root of the problem. This is why one operation is usually followed by another.

In actual fact, the problem lies in our lack of awareness about ourselves, about the subtle relationships between body and mind, self and others. The difficulty we face as a species is our inability to take care of ourselves. Above all, we have the misperception that relaxation will somehow make us *less* safe and effective. This is a sad misunderstanding, because relaxation is the *only* thing that will bring us health, happiness and efficiency on all levels of our being.

That which is tense is under strain and that which is under strain is being weakened. Therefore, learning what relaxation is, how it occurs and how it might be achieved personally, can only be a strengthening experience.

Part One

THE MECHANICS OF THE REFLEX

The mechanics of the reflex

To most people, it probably seems quite obvious that stress is the opposite of relaxation. But is it so obvious what stress actually is?

Stress, as the word is used in this chapter, is to be taken as an undesirable condition. It has nothing to do with excitement or the healthy feeling of being challenged; nor should it be confused with determination, passion or strength. Stress is, in fact, weakness. It is the overloading of the organism. Like a car screaming at its highest revs in first gear, it is not the optimum way of moving forward. Or like the blue-faced boss screaming at his employees, it is not the best way to get things done. Stress is a menacing opponent and one we would do well not to underestimate.

Whilst it is impossible to live in this world without stress, it is possible to develop an immunity to its detrimental effects. With practice, we can learn to handle stressful situations without having our insides all messed up as a result.

But before we can take measures against stress we must learn about it, so that we know exactly what it is that we are dealing with. It is a very popular term, and one that covers a multitude of sins. Kids often say that their parents are stressed-out because they are annoyed about something. Business people call stress the feeling of being under intense pressure.

"Up-tight", "ratty", "bad-tempered", "defensive" and "aggressive" could all be definitions of what we have come to call stress, although terms like depression, fatigue, despondency and suicidal feelings should also be brought under the great stress banner.

Fundamentally, stress occurs when a person loses his or her equilibrium, their "normal functioning". It is a condition that indicates over-stimulation, tension and pressure. And differing personalities react to it in different ways. The common denominator, however, is a feeling that is going in the opposite direction of pleasure and satisfaction. If this feeling persists long enough and strong enough we develop "stress-related symptoms". These commonly take the form of muscular aches and spasms, migraines, insomnia, tics, fatigue syndromes, anxiety attacks and then, if the situation remains unattended, more serious diseases like diabetes, heart disease and cancer can develop. Chronic and severe stress conditions can also degenerate into mental illness.

Clearly, we need a new understanding of stress, but perhaps more importantly a new way of bringing it under control. We need to find a way of becoming familiar with this negative and prevalent force which claims so many people's health and peace of mind. And then, when we can see exactly what it is and what it does, to devise ways to overcome it and reverse its destructive effects.

We need to find a way in which each individual, no matter what his background or state of health, can reliably improve his ability to cope with the stresses and strains of life. Ignorance is no place to begin. Stress has the whole western world tightly in its grip. Statistics show that mental illness, suicides and stress-related diseases are all on a sharp increase. And with the pace of life ever quickening, it is imperative that we discover a better way to deal with our reality.

The Autonomic Nervous System

The most important point to remember about stress is that it is literally a nervous reaction. It occurs within the Autonomic Nervous System (ANS). The ANS is a vast network of nerves branching out from the spinal cord, reaching and directly affecting every organ in the body. It is responsible for maintaining the equilibrium of our internal environment. In fact, it is responsible for anything and everything that we experience automatically.

The sexual urge, as well as the pleasure of its gratification, is manufactured within the ANS. The surge of determination, or dread, when faced with a threatening situation comes from the ANS, as well as the feeling of peaceful contentment that some people are fortunate enough to experience. If you feel it, you feel it with the ANS. All instinctual reactions, such as hunger and sleep, have their home here. Anything commonly called human is likely to have its roots in the ANS. Anything that is universally felt, or known, comes from this place. But, as we are about to see, the ANS is a double-edged sword.

The ANS divides into two distinct systems:

- the Sympathetic Nervous System

- the Parasympathetic Nervous System.

To put their functions simply, read "stressed-out" and "chilled-out" respectively.

Often, nerve fibres from these two systems supply the same organ, one stimulating and the other sedating. They tend to be mutually exclusive, since one system is concerned with the mobilisation of forces to meet an emergency (the famous "fight or flight" response) while the other is to do with the relaxed, regenerative states.

Thus, in a healthy organism, we have these two branches of the ANS maintaining a Yin-and-Yang-type balance.

- The **Sympathetic Nervous System** allows us to deal with stressful situations. Whenever we perceive danger, it will tense our musculature, constrict our blood vessels and speed up our thinking process, amongst numerous other activities. (Note that the word 'sympathetic' in this context refers to the nervous system's reaction to stimuli rather than in its softer, conversational meaning of 'feeling for' another person or situation. The root meaning of the word is, of course, the same.)

- Then, after the danger has passed, the **Parasympathetic Nervous System** will take over, decreasing heartbeat, relaxing blood vessels and clearing away metabolic waste products such as adrenaline and lactic acid.

This is how it should happen: action followed by relaxation; the tide of life ebbing and flowing, expanding and contracting within the ANS.

Health and vitality are the natural result of the harmonic interchange between the Sympathetic and the Parasympathetic. Unfortunately, in our world, this tends to be the exception rather than the rule. In this culture, with all its inherent struggles and strains, people's Sympathetic systems very often stay on guard, unable to give in to the softer, more gentle flows of the Parasympathetic. And if this condition becomes chronic, it can lead to a whole variety of stress-related symptoms and, later, illnesses.

The ANS becomes disturbed and out-of-balance whenever the instinctual response to any situation is denied, be it ignoring our tiredness or overriding our rage. The word instinctual implies something that is automatic, even unconscious. Often we do not have time to work it out, and sometimes it defies analysis. It is simply the way in which we have reacted to this situation.

The way we feel is part of our nature, and we can do ourselves a great disservice by riding roughshod over it too often. We need to remember that we are more than just a conscious choice. We all have a depth of feeling, individual needs, tolerances and preferences. We have the ability for gut feelings as well as analysis. We have a heart as well as a head. For there to be true health there must be a healthy respect for both.

A vivid example of a **healthy nervous system** can be seen in a cat when it comes face to face with a dog. Immediately the Sympathetic goes on red alert. The whole of its body is mobilised in a fraction of a second. Its fur stands on end, it spreads and straightens its legs, it hisses violently and holds the impulse to scratch the dog's eyes out until just the right moment. If the dog has enough sense, it sees the futility of a fight and trots off. With amazing speed the cat then finds somewhere to stretch out and starts licking its fur. The Parasympathetic is now taking over.

For a vivid example of an **unhealthy nervous system** there are few contemporary controversies more pertinent that the Vietnam War. Full of political intrigue and embarrassment from beginning to end, this war was fought in the tropical jungles of the Far East by American conscripts with an average age of 19. To get an idea of what stress can do to the human nervous system, imagine yourself as a 19-year old in fatigues, holding an M16 and standing in the jungles of Vietnam in the 1960s. Your platoon commander is trying to navigate you back to base through a known Viet Cong-infested area.

Booby traps, snipers, deadly snakes - you name it - are lurking around every tree. Picture yourself there. Feel the humid heat clinging to your skin, smell the musky jungle smells mixed in with the scent of Napalm and the whiff of death. Notice how anxious or sick you feel in your stomach, how dry your mouth has become, how weak your knees.

Your attention is alert to screaming pitch.

A thousand thoughts a minute are spraying through your consciousness like machine-gun fire. Your Sympathetic is on full throttle. And in a war zone, it is highly likely to get stuck there. Without a sense of safety, it is almost impossible to let the regenerative and calming powers of the Parasympathetic take over. This is why more Vietnam Veterans killed themselves after they returned home than were killed during the war*, and why so many others litter the mental institutions of America.

Call it Burn-out, call it Nervous Breakdown, call it Post Traumatic Stress Disorder, call it what you will, but it happens when the Sympathetic takes all of the load.

For many people, the business world is something of a war zone. A place where dogs eat dogs, and sharks rule the waves. A competitive environment where only the

---

* In Chuck Dean's book, "Nam Vet", published in 1990 by Multnomah Press, Portland, Oregon, the author states that, "Fifty-eight thousand plus died in the Vietnam War. Over 150,000 have committed suicide since the war ended." According to this book, Chuck Dean is a Vietnam Veteran who served in the 173rd airborne, arriving in Vietnam in 1965. At the time the book was written, Mr Dean was the executive director of Point Man International, a Seattle-based, non-profit support organisation dedicated to healing the war wounds of Vietnam Veterans.

financially fittest survive. This is the jungle that we find ourselves in, trying to sidestep the booby traps and dodge the arrows of misfortune. It is not as powerful a stimulant as war, but in the long run it is equally dangerous. There is an abundance of business people who can never really afford to let their guard down, who never really have the time or ability to relax. They have their indigestions, their bad backs, their heart conditions, but "when needs must, the devil drives" they tell themselves.

Sadly, it is not so much the devil as their own over-active Sympathetic Nervous System that is driving them straight down the fast lane to an early grave. They do not see in their own tics, sleepless nights, stomach knots, palpitations and cold sweating a call to slow down, to take it easy. In their high-flying and sophisticated ways, they do not see the simple truth that for a person to work well he or she must rest well. They do not seem to realise that health requires balance, harmony and equilibrium between body and mind.

The inner life of the body cannot be controlled, it can only be encouraged. If you continually try and make your body do what it doesn't want to do, it will rebel like a slave-uprising. Many people believe, for example, that the common cold is Nature's (or the ANS's) way of slowing us down and releasing accumulated toxins. This would certainly explain why many people feel better than ever after recovering from an illness.

When people are ruled by their Sympathetic Nervous Systems, life slowly becomes more and more uncomfortable.

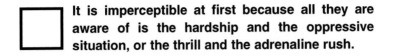

It is imperceptible at first because all they are aware of is the hardship and the oppressive situation, or the thrill and the adrenaline rush.

Over time, if the Sympathetic has the perpetual upper hand, it will slowly become more and more difficult to relax and give in to the Parasympathetic. Once caught in this vicious circle, sleep and appetite become affected. Alcohol and other kinds of suppressants may be sought in a vain attempt to give the sufferer an imitation of what their own Parasympathetic is waiting to give them. Later on, backache may appear, or migraine, repetitive strain injury or peptic ulcer. The list goes on and on, and does not include the different types of mental illness that can result from this unfortunate situation.

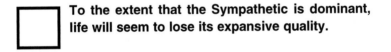

To the extent that the Sympathetic is dominant, life will seem to lose its expansive quality.

Things will feel tighter, harder, more constricted. Alternatively, life may feel dangerously dramatic, explosive, despairing. Either way the various anxiety states will be felt all too keenly. These can be experienced as numbness, palpitations, stomach knots or less easily definable but equally unpleasant sensations. These are all signs that the switch to the Sympathetic Nervous System has got stuck.

If stress is continually layered on top of this block, emotional and digestive disorders can develop. The ANS is out of balance, and therefore is in a weakened state. It no longer has the ability to do its job properly. A crowbar has been jammed between the cogs of its engine. Toxins are not being cleared away, internal combustion has been affected and pressure is building up.

No wonder stress can make us have fantasies about escape and suicidal feelings. *They are no different from thinking about lifeboats when on a sinking ship*.

If we continue to hold on after the Sympathetic has been activated, and after the danger has passed, the Parasympathetic will be unable to take control and restore peace of mind and well-being. This, regrettably, is the norm. We humans are not blessed with the simple life of cats. It is quite common for us to lay awake at night in a silent Sympathetic frenzy worrying about money or the state of our relationship.

If, for whatever reason, the Parasympathetic is *unable* to take over, slowly there becomes a build-up of toxins and stress by-products trapped within the system. The muscles become ever more tense and contracted. This not only happens to the six hundred and twenty skeletal muscles, but also to the smooth musculature that can be found throughout the vast network of tubes within the body systems. The blood vessels as well as the intestines all go into a state of contraction when the Sympathetic is in control.

If, however, the Parasympathetic *is able* to take over, the gateway to another world is opened.

Let's travel gently into the realms of the Parasympathetic: the home of all relaxing, warm and contented feelings. If the Sympathetic is what we need to be in the world, then the Parasympathetic is what we need to be in Heaven. When it is in control, it immediately begins to manufacture a sense of well-being. It brings peace where there was conflict.

Like Mother Nature nourishing her offspring, the Parasympathetic does everything in its power to restore harmony and equilibrium. As it relaxes muscles, blood vessels and internal organs, so the flow of all body fluids becomes easier, smoother, fuller. The intestines expand and the peristalsis (those gurgles of digestion) begins to process the waste products that the Sympathetic has created. It slows the heartbeat and deepens and softens breathing. It calms and changes the brain's waves and patterns, bringing the quieter, more expansive states of mind that are so conducive to imagination and creative thinking.

Slowly, under the right conditions, the Parasympathetic ensures that everything falls or clicks back into place. Everywhere that has been overstretched gets pulled back into line. Everything that has been contracted, begins to expand. And this expansion is experienced as pleasure.

A really good night's sleep is a perfect example. As unusual as it might be for most of us, waking up feeling refreshed from a thoroughly pleasant night's sleep is solely the work of the Parasympathetic.

We move into the Parasympathetic when we have relinquished control, and when the Sympathetic has finished its job, i.e. when we have expended all that energy by fighting or by running as fast as our legs will carry us. However, if we have used up some of the energy, and we are not too stressed-out, the Parasympathetic will do its job while we are watching TV or sleeping.

If you imagine the ANS as an ocean, then the Sympathetic would be the waves, the tides, the storms; while the Parasympathetic would be the ocean's depths, its stillness, its abundance. It is always the power of the Parasympathetic that restores calm to the surface, harmony to the mad ups-and-downs of life. And it is imperative for our survival, let alone our happiness, that we learn to awaken and develop this great healer within.

Holistic therapies

All holistic therapies aim at strengthening the Parasympathetic. There is an army of professional people out there whose purpose is to awaken this all-too-often dormant part of us.

- The **Cranio-sacral Therapist**, with great sensitivity, works directly at unwinding the deep tensions that keep the ANS out-of-balance.

- The **Homeopath**, with her potent little pills, also seeks to restore harmony within the ANS.

- If there is an emotional block, the **Holistic Psychotherapist** works at identifying and resolving the buried conflict within the ANS.

- The **Biodynamic Massage Therapist**, with great flexibility, uses whatever technique is appropriate to harmonise the ANS.

- **Acupuncture, Shiatsu** and most forms of quality massage also have similar effects on the Autonomic Nervous System.

- It is this same system that Yogis seek to purify and manipulate. **Pranayama**, a higher branch of **Hatha Yoga**, is a good example. It has as its goal union with God through breath control. Using highly sophisticated techniques and incredible discipline, devotees work toward strengthening and developing their Parasympathetics to such an extraordinary degree that all the systems and senses of the body become saturated with vitality and well-being. The true potential of the brain is thus harnessed, and consciousness takes several leaps beyond our imagination.

Of course, most of us aren't ready for such spiritual acrobatics. We just want to feel happier and more relaxed; less easily wound-up, less given to worry and more optimistically inclined. Most of us would like to trust in the process of life a little more.

In fact, most of us are looking for a way to relax and be happy, without giving up any of our pleasures and without putting too much effort into it. Fortunately, this is the optimum way to proceed. The Parasympathetic does not respond to denial, or to efforting. Like an abused child cowering under the bed, it needs to be coaxed out of its hiding place. It needs soft words and gentle assurances; a little bit at a time so it is not overwhelmed. It requires the most patient determination. Whatever New Age claims you may have heard, *it is only through the regular and consistent practice of relaxation that the Parasympathetic can be brought back to its former glory.*

As a culture, we have systematically trained ourselves to override the ANS, our instinctual life, in favour of a faster, more "convenient" lifestyle. Unlike the bristling, hissing cat, not many of us give full vent to the Sympathetic. As a race, we tend to be a little frightened of our instinctual reactions. We do not enjoy our heart racing, our hair standing on end, our legs trembling, and so we tend to tense against such disturbing sensations. This often makes us feel in control, and gives the illusion of security. But we are cutting off our nose to spite our face.

If the ANS is inhibited, it will inevitably get stuck in its mode of operation. This does not imply that we should become like animals or small children. It simply means that, in the interest of our health on all levels, *we should respect our feelings*.

Our conscious mind, or head, should be able to overrule the ANS, or heart, because it is not always wise to do exactly what we feel like doing. And this process works fine, so long as the control exerted is relaxed after the stressful situation has passed. The problem comes when this does not occur. When we continue to hold on and to disallow the ANS its natural functioning, stress is the not-so-natural result. When the Sympathetic is activated, it produces a lot of energy which is designed either for fighting the threat, i.e. standing up for ourselves, or for running away from it. It is an animal or instinctual response, and it doesn't matter how rational or intellectual we become, we cannot change the reality of this fact.

Yet how can the natural desire to sleep be honoured when we have to work all the hours God sent and then spend half the night up with the kids? How can we surrender to our bowel movements when there is a long queue in front of the toilet? How can we express the anger and irritation we feel toward our boss when we know it will be cutting off the hand that feeds us? We cannot, and we are not supposed to. Our will power is there for just such emergencies. The healthy use of it is called *deferred gratification*.

It allows us to hold on to the impulse until we find an appropriate place to express it.

It is a gift to have the ability to control the life that is flowing through us. Stress is the abuse of this gift.

Part one in a nutshell

- The Autonomic Nervous System (ANS) is responsible for everything that happens to us automatically.

- The ANS divides into two mutually exclusive systems: the Sympathetic (Fight or flight response) and the Parasympathetic (Relaxation Reflex).

- The ANS becomes disturbed or out of balance whenever the instinctual response to any situation is denied.

- Stress builds up within the body if, for whatever reason, the Parasympathetic is unable to take over.

Part Two

ACTIVATING
THE REFLEX

Activating the reflex

The Relaxation Reflex and the opening of the Parasympathetic are one and the same thing.

"Chilling-out", "unwinding", "calming down", "softening", "melting" and "the opening of the Parasympathetic" are all synonymous terms.

There are many proven methods for opening, or freeing, the Parasympathetic available to us. However, when starting out on these systems it is very wise not to underestimate the grip the Sympathetic can have.

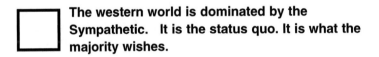

The western world is dominated by the Sympathetic. It is the status quo. It is what the majority wishes.

So, if you live on this planet and you feel stressed-out, unless you take the responsibility for making a change, you're not going to find much support from the world around you. Junk food and drinks are designed to give the Sympathetic a kick-start. The whole economic structure of our society is built on the idea of competition and the use of the Sympathetic, and it can take a great deal of perseverance before you know for sure that a relaxed nervous system has superior functioning in all circumstances. A day here and a day there of doing those things that you can feel help you relax and unwind is not enough. It doesn't take long for us to get sucked back into the Sympathetic environment.

No, we must make a stand. We must commit to our own well-being. Life is too short to spend it in a state of contraction. Vast riches lie dormant within the Parasympathetic system, and can be claimed and owned with persistent practice.

The most effective stress-management technique is simply to do something that makes you feel more relaxed and peaceful, every day. The average person's nervous apparatus has received systematic abuse for many years, and the wisest way to begin to reverse this situation is to realise and fully acknowledge that it's going to take a little while. We all stand in front of a relatively thick wall, and we all have a hammer and chisel.

Some of us run at the wall and hit it as hard as we can. This approach is often painful, and always frustrating. A few of us, meanwhile, see the task for what it is and just get on with it. This approach yields visible progress in only 20-30 minutes.

Remember that for one door of the ANS to open, the other must close. If the Parasympathetic is to come to the fore, the hyped-up Sympathetic must recede. Compared to the action of the Sympathetic, the Parasympathetic is extremely subtle. It is the difference between going round Brands Hatch at 170mph and a stroll through a gladed wood. Consequently, the switch-over can sometimes seem boring or make us feel restless.

This response is quite natural, and is the feeling of the Sympathetic slowing down. It cannot be said too often that we have become accustomed to stress, to life in the fast lane; and moving onto a country lane can make us feel jittery until we get used to it, until we sense the relaxation and notice the beautiful scenery.

Unless happiness comes naturally to us, we need to find something which calms us, slows us down and helps us expand into pleasure. We need some form of daily practice which leaves us feeling more relaxed, more alive and more together. We need some kind of gentle discipline that makes us feel stronger inside. For most of us it is a long-forgotten skill we must relearn, but it is not a skill that can be gained by pumping iron or beating the clock. This monster can only be killed with kindness. We can only slay our dragons with compassion.

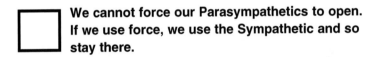

We cannot force our Parasympathetics to open. If we use force, we use the Sympathetic and so stay there.

In the same way that the whole body needs food and sleep, the Parasympathetic needs the right kind of time and space to receive its nourishment. To develop its inherent abilities, the Parasympathetic must be given a chance. Watch how crazy you get if you have to go without food and sleep for a few days.

Stress is Parasympathetic malnutrition.

Everyone needs to find their own way into their Parasympathetic. There are guidelines, which this book seeks to outline, but there is no *one* way. Every branch of every tree twists and turns in a different way.

- The three hours the Dalai Lama spends in daily meditation might not be appropriate for the head of a corporation.

- And the two hours a day that Sting, the rock star, practices yoga may not be possible for a mother of five.

- Some people are able to get their Parasympathetic fix from tending their vegetables or taking afternoon naps.

When choosing a Parasympathetic path, we need to take our personality and our limitations into consideration. If we have a daily practice that makes us feel subtly and consistently better, then that is good enough. It is an accumulative process. We have to progress along this path slowly and surely. We don't want to relax in one go. We want to relax little by little so that the changes to our life apparatus do not disturb the fulfilling of our responsibilities.

Whatever is going on, catastrophe or celebration, we need to continually practice our ability to slow our mind and let our body heal itself. In a few days, weeks or months we will notice another part of ourselves awakening. A part that remains, no matter what is going on; a part that does not move when the storms occur at the surface.

This part of us, our Parasympathetic, responds to the right kind of exercise; and, like a muscle, grows bigger and stronger the more it is used. The beauty of inching forward is that each little step is likely to be stabilised, owned and got-used-to. Steady and gradual growth will produce the healthiest of plants. Both the roots and the branches are more likely to grow at a similar rate.

Imagine the Parasympathetic as a seed, and your commitment to nourishing it as the life-giving water. Day by day you feed the seed, and for a while you don't notice anything. Then, before long, a bright green shoot breaks through the soil, and it gives you the kind of feeling you haven't had since you were a child. It's like magic, and you know exactly how you did it.

To get this advantage in life, all you have to do is to choose amongst the many systems available and pick one that you like and that works for you. You don't have to give up anything, you don't have to lose anything, you just add a healthy practice to your life. You simply make sure that you have a little space, every day, to chill-out. You decide to have a bit of quality time with yourself, every day, even if it means getting up 20mins earlier.

Physical types

If you are a physical type, you might be attracted to one of the many forms of yoga. Any kind of stretching will help rebalance the ANS, so long as it is gentle and enjoyed. All yogic postures are specifically designed to not only soften and lengthen the musculature, but also to calm and strengthen the nervous systems. Movements are generally alternated so as to stretch the spinal column forwards and backwards, thus freeing this most important centre of nervous activity from the constrictions and pressures that everyday living has placed upon it.

People who practice yoga every day report huge improvements in their complexion, stamina, energy, state of mind and well-being. It is a tried and tested system of exercise which has proven extremely effective in producing the kind of results we are looking for, for thousands of years. There is an abundance of books on the subject, and classes in every town where you can get professional support and tuition.

Alternatively, Tai Chi, or one of its derivatives such as Qi Kung, may suit you better. Just as authentic as yoga, these movements and exercises from China work toward bringing the mind and body into ever greater harmony. Slow, flowing movements calm the mind and stimulate the Parasympathetic. Exponents of this type of exercise report increased efficiency in all areas of their lives.

Advanced students talk of an exquisite feeling of oneness with Nature. Tai Chi and associated exercises have been practiced and developed over thousands of years. They have an amazing repertoire of movements and techniques for releasing every kind of tension known to man, and woman.

Mental types

If you are a mental type, you might feel drawn to one of the hundreds of meditation techniques available. Ever since Moses went up the mountain, or Buddha sat under the tree, people have been devising ways to still the jabber, and enter more peaceful and productive states of mind.

It is exactly this overstimulation of the brain that we need to quieten if we are to enter the Parasympathetic. When the mind is stilled, the body becomes peaceful and the Parasympathetic takes over. And as it takes over, it not only relaxes our whole being but also purifies and nourishes all the systems of the body. It is, therefore, quite possible to achieve vibrant health by doing absolutely nothing!

Transcendental Meditation (TM) is probably the most widely used meditation technique in the western world, and it is certainly the most widely researched. The TM organisation has volume upon volume of results from scientifically controlled research. They have found, amongst many other things, that people who use TM every day for five years have 60-70% fewer illnesses than people who do not (*Scientific Research on Transcendental Meditation*, an introduction and overview, January 1998).

After reading some of the research, it makes one wonder why everyone is not willing to give up 30 or 40 minutes a day for such amazing results. It would be interesting to calculate how much time those 60-70% of illnesses would have taken up, and then compare it to the time given to a daily discipline.

Whatever turns your Parasympathetic on!

Shop around, experiment, try things out. You're looking for a technique you like, that calms you, relaxes you, makes you feel good. You don't have to join a religion or get mystical (unless, of course, you want to) you just have to learn how to make yourself feel better.

Here are a few ways you can make yourself feel better right now, or as soon as you have a bit of space. A few exercises follow which you might want to choose from and use as your daily discipline, or experiment with until you find something that suits you better. Each represents a doorway into the Parasympathetic, and it is recommended that you taste them and find the one or ones that you like best, that bring you the most pleasure. Do ONE at a time, and then give yourself a few hours to notice the effects.

It will not help if you do more than one at a time, because you will have trouble knowing which gave you what effect. As you slowly learn from your results, you will have a better idea of your personal needs.

These exercises should be practiced with gentleness and a respect for your current limitations. They are all designed to take you out of the Sympathetic and into the Parasympathetic. Remember that the more pleasure you experience while doing them the more they will work for you.

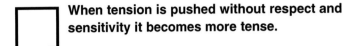 **When tension is pushed without respect and sensitivity it becomes more tense.**

The body needs a loving attitude to get it to relax and unwind, and we achieve this by finding where we are tense, then stretching that place a millimetre at a time. Only in this way can we safely and pleasurably expand and let go of the tensions which imprison our sense of well-being. If you watch our friend the cat stretch, you will have a fine role model. Or if you remember a time when you woke up from a sleep or nap and had a spontaneous and satisfying reach for the sky, this is the way it should be practiced.

The popular phrase, "No pain, no gain" should be completely and utterly forgotten for the sake of these exercises. In fact, the opposite is true. If there is no pleasure, there will be no gain.

It must also be remembered that most of us are not as aware of our bodies as we think we are. Chronic muscular tensions not only shorten the muscles but also prohibit feeling in them. Because of this condition it can be only too easy to injure ourselves. When we do a strenuous exercise, we put those shortened muscles under a lot of stress without being able to truly feel what we are doing. This often results in damage to the muscle, as well as a fair amount of frustration to our new plans for health and happiness.

It is precisely because of these deep, underlying tensions that the best exercises are the subtle ones. When we manage to produce a fine pleasure where we could not feel one before, we have expanded our comfort zone, we have deepened our capacity for pleasure and we have grown in consciousness.

In the long run, slow, flowing movements will always produce more well-being than fast or forced ones. As we practice these exercises, particularly the breathing ones, it is important to acknowledge our emotional state.

As will be described more fully in part three, the breath is the vehicle for the emotions, and when we expand our breathing we not only take in more vitality but we are also able to feel our feelings more fully. If we can make friends with these feelings (more about this in part four), they will cease to trouble us and we can let go of them on the exhale. Generally speaking, they are only a problem because we are anxious or unable to feel them deeply.

The exercises that follow have been chosen for their simplicity and accessibility. In any one of them, you could find what you are looking for, or you may find that they simply whet your appetite for something more.

Do ONE at a time, and then give yourself a few hours to notice the effects.

- Deep breathing

- Tensing and relaxing

- Alternate nostril breathing

- Charging the legs

- The great Tai Chi breathing circle

Deep Breathing

If you're the type of person who finds it difficult to switch off the chatter in your head, you'll probably need some type of definite focus to keep it busy while you learn to relax. And if you can find a practice that combines this approach with an exercise for the body, you've struck gold. An excellent exercise for body, mind and soul is as follows:

> Lie down somewhere very comfortable and quiet. Gently inhale to the count of nine and then gently exhale to the count of nine. (This may be difficult at first because stress quite literally shortens the breath, but it will expand with a gentle persistence).

Try this for 20 minutes and you will be pleasantly surprised by how it calms and clears your mind and makes your body feel relaxed and energised. Slowing and deepening the breathing in this way not only slows the mind but also relaxes the body. Through the counting, the mind becomes focused on the slow, deep and rhythmic expansion and contraction of the Parasympathetic Nervous System. Worrying thoughts begin to drift away, and troublesome feelings slowly rise and integrate.

Tensing and Relaxing

Another remarkably simple method for learning how to relax is to get yourself into a comfortable position and then tense every muscle in your body for a few seconds. Really try to tense everything, including your thinking, and then completely relax your grip, noticing as you do all the different sensations in your body. This basic procedure should be repeated as many times as is necessary to get a real sensation of relaxation.

Tensing and relaxing is a highly practical way to learn the difference between the Sympathetic and Parasympathetic, between contraction and expansion. The more you practice the more you become aware of the difference, and the more aware you are the more choice you have.

Alternate Nostril Breathing

Alternate nostril breathing is an incredibly simple and equally efficient exercise that can be found in most books about yoga. It is used to purify the Nadis, a Hindu word for nerve endings. Whilst its effects are rather subtle at first it has a marked tendency to make its user feel both stronger and more relaxed. This makes perfect sense because it clears blockages and nourishes the nervous system.

It is often called the Calming Breath or the Purifying Breath. Some books claim that it effectively balances the two hemispheres of the brain.

The way to practice Alternate Nostril Breathing is to close your right nostril with the thumb of your right hand and inhale gently through the left.

Then close the left nostril and exhale through the right. Keeping the left nostril closed inhale through the right.

Then close the right nostril and exhale through the left. You have now completed one round.

Some texts say that nine of these are sufficient for one day, some say it should be practiced until you feel tired, while others say you should breathe like this at your normal depth and rhythm for five minutes per day.

Experiment, and see which works best for you. Try a different way each day, and let your results guide you.

Charging the Legs

If we are feeling anxious or overwhelmed, very often our legs have become tense and our feeling of support and contact with the ground has been undermined. This is hardly surprising since we routinely sit down on the way to work, sit down all day, sit down on the way home and then sit in front of the television all night.

If we are not conscious of the strength in our legs it will most probably be difficult or anxiety provoking to stand up for ourselves. This condition usually manifests itself as a feeling of weakness in the legs or no feeling at all. Happily, there are many simple and rapid remedies for this situation. Here is one.

Stand with your feet shoulder width apart and toes pointing outward. Now, as you inhale go down into a squat. Then stand up as you exhale.

Try and do 20 of these, but stop as soon as it ceases to feel good - always bear your comfort and pleasure in mind. (If you have a build-up of tension in your lower back or legs, squats may not work for you. Instead, try walking up and down a flight of stairs a few times. Alternatively, you can put all the weight of your body on one bended knee for a minute or two, and then swap over).

By now the muscles in your legs should be gorged with blood and your breath should have opened into your pelvis somewhat.

Next stand with your feet 12-14 inches apart, toes pointing inward and knees slightly bent. Try and relax into your pelvis and let it "sit" on top of your legs. As you allow yourself to breathe easily you should notice some kind of tremor or trembling in your legs. The technical term for this trembling is Clonism, and it is the tension in the muscles being released. Stand in this way for a couple of minutes and you will have completed this exercise.

Waking up the legs can take a lot of pressure off the ANS, and stimulate the Parasympathetic. It is an excellent and very healthy way to start the day, as well as an effective first-aid treatment for any kind of anxiety or overwhelm.

The Great Tai Chi Breathing Circle

As the name implies, this exercise is borrowed from the vast repertoire of ingenious movements that make up the system of Tai Chi and its offshoots. It stands on its own as an excellent daily practice that is sure to give us the results we are looking for. If it is done correctly, it will enhance your sense of grounding and energy flow as well as opening the chest, diaphragm and all the breathing muscles.

As with all these exercises it will give you more energy and more relaxation at the same time. The procedure to follow is this:

Stand with your hands by your side, feet shoulder width apart and knees slightly bent; try to give yourself a good, solid stance on the ground.

Next, as you slowly inhale bring your straightened arms outward and upward to a place above your head. The back of your hands should meet above your head, thus forming a circle.

As you exhale, slowly bring your hands, palms facing the ground, down the front of your body.

Your hands should be parallel to each other, and you should visualise gently pushing energy down to the ground.

When your exhale comes to its end, your hands will come to rest by your sides, where they begun. You have completed a breathing circle.

Try doing five or ten circles to begin with, then rest and do another set, each time trying to make them deeper and slower. Gradually build up to as many as feels good to you. After a while, you will notice the very pleasurable sensation of effortlessness as your arms seem to go up by themselves.

After practicing any of these exercises, it can be very beneficial to lie down and focus your attention on the new sensations that have been produced. If you simply lie still for 5-10 minutes and feel what you're feeling with curiosity, as opposed to apprehension, you will be relaxing.

In any endeavour, success is achieved by regularly and repeatedly doing what works. Find something that makes you feel better, more relaxed, more expansive, more peaceful, and make it the habit of a lifetime.

The mind and the body come together in this practice. As the mind relaxes so does the body. And as the body relaxes so does the mind. This is a circle that is not vicious at all, but endlessly kind to all levels of our being. For when mind and body stop fighting one another, they can live in peace.

This is the quiet place where Nature takes over, where her magical fingers massage all the tensions away. This is the great melting pot where the remains of the day can be poured, where those trying thoughts, crazy ideas and fantastic notions can be laid to rest and filed away.

Notice how your Parasympathetic practice makes you feel from day to day, from week to week, and then imagine how you might feel in five years from now if you have that kind of improvement every day. We can change our lives, but it must come slowly and surely. Fireworks burn out very quickly; and great highs are often followed by equally large lows.

Inching forward may be a little frustrating at first, but

in the long run patient persistence will yield the greatest prize. As the great chinese philosopher, Confucius, said,

> *"Patience is the key to joy, and haste is the key to sorrow."*

Part two in a nutshell

- Stress is Parasympathetic malnutrition.

- The most effective stress-management technique is simply to do something that makes you feel more relaxed and peaceful every day.

- When tension is pushed without respect or sensitivity is becomes more tense.

- We have to find what turns our Parasympathetic on; what makes us feel more relaxed, more peaceful, more together and stronger inside.

- Success is achieved by regularly and repeatedly doing what works.

Part Three

THE REFLEX
AND YOUR BODY

The reflex and your body

As we gain familiarity and skill with the Relaxation Reflex, the body takes on a new feel, a new sheen. To the extent which we cease to treat it quite so harshly, it begins to **respond** rather than **rebel**.

When we allow the tensions to unwind, our bodily awareness deepens. And as we take it into our confidence so it, too, begins to share its deeper secrets with us. Through the body's healthy guidance, we begin to learn how to give ourselves what we need. We slowly learn to be aware of our needs before they reach boiling point, before they start screaming at us. We begin to find harmony between head and heart, between mind and body. This is a deep, subtle process that ends with the happy realisation that being in your body is the best possible place to be.

Unfortunately, many of us are only dimly aware of the home in which we live. Instead, we spend most of our time either loitering in the past or racing into the future, both of which are realms outside of the body. Present time is often uncomfortable, and consequently, we do not feel our pain and joy in the here and now. The pain is kept in the past as some form of wound or grievance that has been neither healed nor forgiven, while the joy is in some achievement which we are fervently hoping for, desperately working toward. To be truly in the present moment, i.e. fully conscious, we necessarily need to be in touch with our body sensations.

Anyone who excels at anything FEELS what he or she is doing. Full concentration, and therefore maximum efficiency, has nothing left over to keep in the past or place in the future, it requires absolutely everything right now.

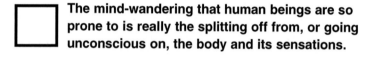

The mind-wandering that human beings are so prone to is really the splitting off from, or going unconscious on, the body and its sensations.

This reaction to reality is fostered and actively encouraged by society, with all its many, many images of the perfect body and the perfect composure. It is part of human nature that, when we continually fail to reach a standard, either placed there by us or by people we want to please, there comes a resignation, a disassociation. It simply becomes too painful to keep trying to reach an impossible goal.

Often imperceptibly, we reject our bodies before they are put on the reject pile, according to, and administered by, the carefully planned whims of society. But then corporations and their advertising agencies are not interested in the truth. They are concerned only with manipulating our insecurities to sell their products. It is as if the ideal is for us all to become like the rows of perfectly cloned and shiny fruits in the supermarket.

Yet the way a body looks from the outside is but one

facet of a whole diamond. The richness of a body lies in its depth of feeling, not whether it meets the criteria of the latest fad. Every single pleasurable activity that we can experience is a pleasurable activity primarily because it causes us to have pleasure in our bodies. The most glorious victory, as well as the most crushing defeat, is experienced with the body, in the body. There is no getting away from it. Every experience we have while we are alive is had with the body. And so, the more relaxed and open the body is, the richer our experience of life will be.

A body of evidence

Within the English Language is a wealth of evidence which suggests just how essential our physical experience is to us. Body language abounds in our speech and vocabulary; physical phrases with emotional meanings litter our conversation. So, *prick up your ears, keep your eyes peeled* and see if you can *digest* the following examples.

> Most of us are capable of being *big-headed*, of being *headstrong* or of *putting our head in the sand* to avoid really looking at a problem. If we go *out of our head* or get in *over our head*, we can always *get our head down*, or even *put our heads together* with a friend and solve the problem. Once the solution is found we might *throw our heads back* in laughter or *hold our heads high* with pride or even *have our head in the clouds.*
>
> But it is the eyes that say it all. We *look down* at some people and *look up to* others. We *look daggers* when

we feel hatred, we *look for trouble* when we behave rashly and we can *look a person in the eye* when we have nothing to hide. We can *see reason*, we can *see red*, we can *see eye to eye* with someone, we can *see through* them and we can *see them off.*

The fact that all our experience comes to us through our bodies is as *plain as the nose on our face.* And this prominent appendage is rich in metaphors. When we *follow our nose* we may be quicker to *smell a rat*, or *smell if something is a bit fishy.* If we want to *keep our nose clean*, we *keep our nose to the grindstone. We look down them, turn them up, put them out of joint and cut them off to spite our face.*

To continue our bio-logical discussion, getting it *in the neck* will frequently give us a *pain in the neck*, not to mention a *headache* or a *pain in the arse.* And the act of swallowing obviously holds more for us than just the ingestion of food. How many times have we been forced to *swallow our words* or our pride?

If that seems like a lot of functioning, how about the shoulders? This is the part of the body generally considered as capable of bearing responsibility, a burden or blame, or of providing comfort, i.e. giving someone *a shoulder to cry on.*

The arms, hands and fingers are no less rich in symbolism. These parts of our body are responsible for giving and taking, embracing and resisting. We keep a person *at arm's length*, or greet them *with open arms.* We *grab hold* of something or *push it away.* We *lend a hand*, or *walk hand in hand* with friends or loved ones. In the workplace, things are generally *in hand* or *out of hand*. And when things do get out of hand we sometimes *point the finger* at someone else; usually because we feel we have *worked our fingers to the bone*, only to let the opportunity slip through those same digits.

We also use body parts to designate character traits. For example, someone with *no backbone* will hardly have a *chest bursting with pride*. People who *hang their head in shame* or despair are most unlikely to have a *spring in their step*. Someone who is *tight-lipped, tight-fisted* or *tight-arsed* is unlikely to have a *good belly laugh*. We often describe someone who has the courage of their conviction, a person who has the strength to *follow their gut reaction* or instinct, as *gutsy*. And if this instinct really *rubs us up the wrong way*, or *gets our back up*, we may end up *hating their guts*.

This physical orientation is important because as we progress with the Relaxation Reflex, we begin to inhabit our humanity more fully. As we learn how to relax and let our Parasympathetics take over, our feelings flow more easily. Our consciousness is no longer crammed into our head, but more evenly distributed through the whole of us. In other words, our bodies become more animated as the tensions begin to unwind. Life begins to flow through us more fully and more freely. Our feelings as well as our sense of identity grow subtly stronger and healthier.

Sexuality

And since our sexuality is such a primal and fundamental

part of us, this natural urge may become stronger and healthier also. At the bottom of the belly and in between the top of the legs is an area of the body that is positively loaded with double meanings. When this part of the body is strongly attracted to the same area in another, it can move Heaven and Earth. What dangles or disappears in this place is solely responsible for the survival of the human race. No wonder it carries with it such ardent desire or such depravity. (Interestingly enough, this function is controlled by the Parasympathetic and, therefore, inhibited by the Sympathetic. This fact readily explains why stress can and does effect sexual performance). When this area is aroused, and the feeling is allowed to flow through the heart, we have a condition which most people have spent a considerable amount of time contemplating, fantasizing and dreaming about.

Romantic love makes our hearts heave, our breasts flutter, our imaginations soar. It can fill our hearts with happiness, or break them as easily. It is rocket fuel to the human condition. And its satisfaction or dissatisfaction can cause extreme bliss or jealous rage, or just about anything in between.

It is thoroughly uncanny how something with such an incredible charge around it can receive such a total sweeping under the carpet by parents and society in general. When this energy begins to move in puberty, its denial causes untold suffering. Spotty faces and taut tummies frequently come from the pushing down of this most natural and basic desire. Is it any wonder that there is such clumsiness and insecurity when the time finally comes to part with our virginity?

Last, but by no means least, the legs and feet carry a lot more than just the weight of the body. They form the support of our whole structure and represent our *standing in the world*. If someone is *hung-up* or *up-in-the-air*, it means that they do not *have their feet on the ground*. Such people are out of touch with reality, they are generally anything but *down-to-earth*. Like a tree without its roots, these people are blown away every time a strong wind comes along.

The legs have another, often overlooked, function. They are responsible for exiting excess energy from the organism. Anyone who has felt their legs tremble, or has tried the exercise suggested in part two, will have experienced this phenomenon. The body is an energetic system, and like an electrical system, it must be earthed if it is to avoid burn-out. When the Sympathetic goes on red alert, it not only causes energy in the form of feeling to race up the body but also pours it down the legs and into the ground.

If we do not make a stand, run or allow our legs to tremble, ALL this energy must come upwards. Exactly the same thing happens in any electrical apparatus. If too much energy comes into the appliance, and it has no earth through which to discharge, it will explode. This accurately describes what can happen in our emotional system.

Like the mouth and the arms, the genitals and legs are powerful avenues of expression. If the legs, as well as the genitals, are tense and blocked to the flow of feeling, all that emotion will start coming upward. If the tension above is less than the tension below, we'll experience it as frustration or anxiety, or as pressure and discomfort in the stomach. If the tension above is equal to the tension below, we will only be dimly aware, probably too lost in our depression to care.

Most of us learnt as children to tense and straighten our knees, and to control those horribly weak, trembly legs. How many times have we quashed the impulse to run and forced ourselves to stand still? How many of us were stopped from stamping, stopped from kicking, stopped from playing with our beautiful genitalia?

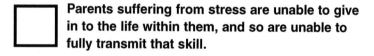

Parents suffering from stress are unable to give in to the life within them, and so are unable to fully transmit that skill.

This is why we must take the responsibility to teach it to ourselves. And because the misinformation that we have received goes so far back and goes down so deep, we need a vigorous daily commitment to rectify the situation. For most people, there is a considerable amount of body awareness to be reclaimed from the clutches of muscular tension. But we can learn to activate the Relaxation Reflex on progressively deeper levels, if we patiently persevere, and if we realise that it can only help every area of our lives.

As we begin to release and relax the rigidities in our legs, we will find it easier and more pleasurable to stand on our own two feet; and allow them to support us and maintain a good relationship with reality. And as we allow ourselves to unwind some of the moralistic muscular attitudes in and around our genitalia, so will we increasingly enjoy and appreciate Nature's little, and sometimes not so little, steam valve.

But the singing of the birds and the humming of the bees is not all that goes on within us. Emotions are moving through our veins and arteries. Fear makes our *blood run cold*, anger makes our *blood boil* and passion makes us *full-blooded*. The heart *skips a beat* in love, but if this love is lost it is *torn in two*. The heart is universally recognised as the feeling centre of the human being. Throughout history it has been associated with love and the deepest, truest part of us.

As a man thinketh in his heart, so is he.

Hearts can be made of gold or stone, depending on whether the owner has a generous or cruel nature. We can have our *hearts in our mouths*, or they can be *in the right place*. It just depends on how we're feeling at the time. And feelings never come to order. Sometimes they fill us instantaneously, sometimes they lurk around the edge of consciousness and sometimes we think we are feeling one thing but it turns out to be something else.

Some women cry instead of expressing their rage. Conversely, a lot of men experience their anxiety as anger or aggression, often frightened to feel the vulnerability that the situation warrants. Feelings can be stuck or blocked, they can be flowing or frozen. But they are always valid, no matter where they come from, and no matter how they are felt.

Some people are emotionally dramatic by nature. They

have their feelings quickly, and they are as quickly gone. Others, meanwhile, have a quieter and slower way of feeling their emotions. Each is as authentic and as legitimate as the other.

Temperature changes, movements and sensations are also plentiful within the human body. We have the burning of anger or desire, and the coldness of fear or hatred. We have the warmth of enthusiasm and the cool of reserve. We may quiver, shake, tremble, jump, heave, retch, sink, melt, become gooey or hardened. We can get goosebumps, shivers, pins and needles, become bloated, empty, constricted, relaxed, to name but a few. With so much going on it seems strange indeed that we manage to feel bored.

In fact, boredom, like depression and many of the anxiety states, comes from the cutting off or pushing down of the flow of feeling within our bodies. Boredom implies a lack of feeling. And as we have seen, it is very difficult for a body to feel nothing at all. Next time you get bored try taking ten deep breaths into the top of your chest, and then watch what happens to your boredom.

It is impossible to breathe deeply and not intensify the sensations and feelings in our body. Aside from other reasons which we will be covering shortly, the increase in oxygen intake will accelerate all activity within the organism. Fresh, oxygenated blood cells will inundate everything from the top of our heads to the tips of our toes. The deeper we breathe the more energy we take in, and the more nourished our nervous systems become.

Breathing attitudes are central to stress, as well as the

Relaxation Reflex, and a better understanding of this pivotal process can only help us master both more easily. Stress is caused by the holding back of natural feeling impulses. It is caused by the continual denial of our inner needs which the body communicates to us all the time. These impulses or needs can only be held back by the tensing of the musculature and the inhibition of the breathing mechanism. You will never see a tense person breathe fully and freely.

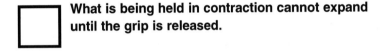

What is being held in contraction cannot expand until the grip is released.

And we cannot just suddenly let go of what we are barely conscious of. We have got used to our shallow breathing, grown accustomed to not being really sure what we are feeling. Colds, hay fever, snoring, asthma and other afflictions of the breathing apparatus are normal to us. The breathing attitudes of Victorian women in corsets are still prevalent, though not quite so obvious. Women still tend to breathe into the upper chest, while men tend to breathe into their bellies. This may well explain why women are inclined to be more emotional and men have more of an inclination toward power. One tends to have more heart and the other more guts.

Physically speaking, this divide between man and woman is rooted in the diaphragm, that great sheet of muscle that separates the chest from the abdomen, and whose rhythmic expansion and contraction is responsible for air coming in and out of our lungs. When this part of us has become chronically tense we will either breathe into the chest *or* the belly. This tension precludes us from allowing the breath, or our feelings, to really fill us up, or to really travel through us. The result is that women often lack power and men often lack soft feelings. In this instance, it cannot be said that either man or woman is right or wrong. Ideally, we should all have both.

Wilhelm Reich, the very great pioneer of psychosomatic medicine, describes this widespread problem in his fascinating book, *The Function of the Orgasm.*

"Respiratory inhibition and the fixation of the diaphragm is doubtlessly one of the first and most important acts in suppressing pleasurable sensations in the abdomen, as well as curtailing "abdominal anxiety" ... almost all patients remember that as children they held down and suppressed these sensations in the upper abdomen which are felt quite intensely in anger or anxiety. They learned to do this spontaneously by holding their breath and pulling in their abdomen."

The breath is the vehicle of the emotions

We sigh with exasperation, we snort with frustration, we gasp with exhaustion or astonishment, we breathe easy in safety, we pant in passion and we take a lungful in love. And the easiest way to stop ourselves from feeling an emotion is to stop breathing. If you really pay attention to your breathing through a 24 hour period, you will be amazed by how many times you do hold your breath. Everything that makes you jump through the day, everything that challenges or confronts you and everything that makes you feel uncomfortable will take its toll on your breathing. If you were simply to practice one of the breathing exercises in the previous chapter regularly, your ability to relax would increase and your stress would decrease, dramatically.

Breathing is one way in which we expand and contract all the time, and the rhythmic pulsation of the heart and circulatory system is another. The heart pumps blood through the arteries to all the tissues of the body. When the energy and nourishment that it carries has been deposited in the tissues, the blood returns to the heart via the veins, thus completing a pulsation through the body.

It is the Autonomic Nervous System that is responsible for the intensity and direction of that flow, as we can see from the colour of someone's face when they are blowing a fuse. It does this by opening and closing blood vessels in various parts of the body. Elsworth Baker, in his book *Man in the Trap*, takes this idea a stage further when he says:

> "This energy flow is felt as emotion. For example, rage results when energy flows into the muscles; pleasure, identical to expansion, results when energy flows to the skin surface (the genitals are part of the skin or ectoderm); and anxiety follows if the flow of energy is to the internal organs and therefore causes contraction of the organism."

Elsworth Baker goes on to cover the subject of energy flow to the skin in more depth, and here he talks about his teacher, Wilhelm Reich:

"Reich believed that, in pleasure, there was an electrical charge at the skin surface and he set out to investigate. He used an oscillograph and found that there actually was a charge. The greater the pleasure, the higher the charge that showed on the oscillograph. Furthermore, in unpleasurable situations the charge disappeared. Here was concrete evidence of a real energy ... Later he showed that this energy radiated out beyond the skin surface as an energy field".

Reich's findings strongly imply that pleasure and a healthy glow are identical. His discoveries also ably explain why stress, or contraction, is devoid of pleasure. It follows quite naturally that the antidote for stress is a feeling of expansion, or physical pleasure. It is curious, therefore, that physical pleasure has collected such bad press over the ages. And all the more curious that some of us associate the mortification of the flesh with the attainment of Heaven, asceticism and self-denial with holiness. How is it possible to come closer to the Creator of Life by suppressing or killing Life in the body?

Of course, excess is no closer to the truth. Great excess will always be a symptom of neurosis, and it will never take very long to spot the price that has to be paid for it. The key to activating the Relaxation Reflex does not reside in either extremes. It lies in the incredibly simple practice of doing things which make our bodies feel relaxed and pleasurable. This practice will also help us develop the habit of being pleasure-led - a characteristic of emotional health and a necessity for the healthy management of stress.

Once we know how to maintain our inner sense of well-being we become a lot less desperate and dependent. This independent well-being is the strength we need to meet the world.

Paradoxically, when we are in pleasure, we are unaware of our bodies. Instead, we are completely identified with what we are enjoying. This is the time when the pressure quite literally gets taken off our insides. We become unaware of the tensions and limitations that we thought of as our bodies. Pleasure is not a constriction, it is an outward moving sensation, an expanding and unifying feeling. The experience of pleasure in our tissues lets us know that we are getting away from the ravages of stress. Expansive and flowing sensations tell us that we have come through the trial, that we are now letting go of the fear and letting life flow once again.

Healthy pleasure makes us feel good as a whole. It is not the relief of satisfying a craving from one part of us.

Real pleasure is experienced as a cohesive force that holds us together. It unifies all the scattered parts of us, and brings us into one pleasurable focus. As our awareness opens in this way, it becomes easier to recognise other avenues of pleasure. In terms of releasing bodily tension, this is the optimum way to proceed. This is the path that does not pummel chronic muscular tension, but allows pleasure to melt the rigidities and let new life in.

Or as Bob Mandel, author of *Open Heart Therapy*, put it:

"Pleasure is God's love."

Part three in a nutshell

- Activating the Relaxation Reflex allows feelings to flow more easily.

- All feelings are valid and appropriate.

- Pleasure is an expansion, and pain is a contraction.

- Real pleasure makes us feel good as a whole.

- Wholesome pleasure is health.

Part Four

THE REFLEX
AND YOUR MIND

The reflex and your mind

The part of our anatomy that we associate with the mind is, of course, the head. Despite the fact that active intelligence is present everywhere in the body, we generally consider that the brain does our thinking for us. This idea certainly has validity, but what we tend to overlook is the influence the ANS exerts over our brain and therefore our thinking.

As we have seen in previous chapters, when the Sympathetic gets activated through real or perceived threat, it precludes peaceful, expansive and pleasurable thinking. If some person or experience shocks us, emotionally charged images can enter our heads fast and furiously.

Imagine walking down a darkened street at night, for example. Suddenly, two tom cats start a squealing, screaming fight just behind you. As in part one, the Sympathetic immediately goes on red alert, and as it does so, it throws related images at our mind's eye. Maybe we see a stalker, a mugger, a monster waiting to pounce. For each person, the images are different, but the quality of them is the same. *They are proof that the Sympathetic is active on a mental level*.

The brain functions in a very similar way to the solar

plexus when it becomes charged and contracted in an emergency situation. Our thoughts and images turn into adrenaline-crazed phantoms. Our thinking becomes tense and agitated, and our perception of the world can become dramatically affected. If this sudden updrift of energy does not find expression and/or relaxation, there comes a build-up of worrying thoughts.

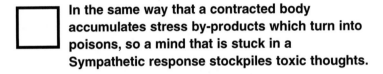

In the same way that a contracted body accumulates stress by-products which turn into poisons, so a mind that is stuck in a Sympathetic response stockpiles toxic thoughts.

Imagination as well as memory are essentially neutral. They can be utilised by the Sympathetic or the Parasympathetic. Understandably, the Sympathetic has a strong tendency to both remember and imagine the worst, because by its very nature it is always in danger. While the Parasympathetic has a built-in bias toward the good and the happy, because its function is to relax, expand and regenerate. The nature and quality of our thoughts change according to which branch of the ANS has the upper hand.

A nervous reaction to a shock or a threat will give rise to shocking or fearful images. An angry or defensive response will create angry or defensive thoughts. Whereas a feeling of unwinding or melting will produce thoughts and images of an expansive or pleasurable nature. The activation of the Relaxation Reflex tends to make our thinking more hopeful and confident.

The body/mind continuum

When life is moving in our bodies we **feel**, and when life is moving in our heads we **think.** Thinking and feeling are not separate circuits. One feeds into the other. The ANS not only informs our thinking but also our thinking has a powerful influence over the ANS. The way in which we think has a direct connection to the way we feel. The manner in which we interpret the information coming to us can be the difference between stress and relaxation. As we shall see, it is not what happens to us so much as the way we perceive it that makes all the difference.

Impressions flood the human consciousness constantly. They come through our skin, eyes, ears, taste buds, nostrils and from the vast network of nerves running through every internal and external organ of the body. They come to us in the shape of dreams, memories, brainwaves, fantasies. But it is not, generally, until they have been collated, or made sense of, by the conscious mind that they are referred to as perceptions. As the word is used in everyday language, perception actually means a personal interpretation of impressions received.

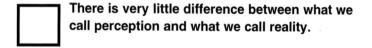

There is very little difference between what we call perception and what we call reality.

We perceive reality according to our learning, our experience and our emotional state. And because our learning is never complete, our experience never ending and our emotional state never the same, perception is apt to change. Few people these days perceive the world as flat, nor man's landing on the moon as an impossibility. Nowadays we see locomotives and 747s, not iron horses and iron birds. And the way a child perceives reality changes radically as he or she grows up. Only the odd adult sees a monster in the shadow on his bedroom wall. Generally speaking, logic overpowers imagination with the passing of years, but logic does not always overpower emotion.

Fear and anger, as well as love, are more than capable of distorting our perception. When we find out in a dramatic and painful way that our perception has been faulty, we say that our illusions have been shattered. What we had taken for granted turns out to be wrong. This can be very traumatic, and can threaten our sanity, for what we assumed to be reality is suddenly ripped away from under our feet.

Conversely, a similar kind of shift in perception can bring about great joy and elation in us. This is often called seeing the light. It happens when our perception has been stuck in a particularly unpleasant way of seeing things, i.e. an insoluble problem, an insurmountable obstacle. Then, suddenly, we become aware of a solution or a way out. This answer very often comes to us out of the blue, when we least expect it. The result is that our perception takes a sudden shift and our reality changes in the twinkling of an eye.

Either experience, painful or pleasurable, soon teaches us that neither perception nor reality are static phenomena.

It is possible to divide perception into two basic

components: **content** and **context**. Content is **what** we perceive, while context is the **way** we perceive it. For example, the content of one perception could be 10 fluid ounces of water in a pint glass, and the context of that perception could either be a half full or half empty glass of water.

Positive or pleasurable contexts have a strong tendency to activate the Relaxation Reflex, or Parasympathetic; whereas negative or fearful contexts tend to stimulate the Sympathetic.

If the contents of one's lunch were sheep's eyeballs and ram's testicles, most people would put them into a negative context, yet there are people in the Middle East who would put that dish into a highly positive context.

Let's stay in the Middle East for our next example. Sir Richard Burton, the great explorer, was once sitting with a sheikh and his entourage eating lunch when one of the Sheikh's wives arrived on a camel. As she began to dismount she slipped and fell to the ground. Her skirts floated upward, her legs were thrown to either side and her genitalia were exposed to all and sundry. After she had regained her modesty and things had become normal once again, Sir Richard turned to his host and asked him if he was upset by what had just happened. The Sheikh brushed his question aside by saying that his wife's face had remained covered so what did it matter.

One man's succulent filet steak is another man's poison. Some people hold the experience of taking a cold shower on a winters morning in a positive context. Some people like to eat the hottest possible curry. And it seems certain that someone, somewhere, enjoys going to the dentist. Body piercing is another case in point. There are religious sects in the Philippines and India which, around Eastertide, practice self-flagellation and half-day crucifixions. It cannot be difficult to understand that without a positive context to hold their bloody practices in, these people would be quite insane.

Clearly, it is possible to hold just about anything in a positive context, if one has a mind to do so. It is not the experience so much as the way in which we see or interpret the experience that dictates our emotional response. The Sympathetic Nervous System will not react to a shadow unless we see an axe-murderer in it. If someone bumps into us, we will not become angry unless we see it as deliberate. It is the context in which we place any given experience that gives us the feeling of that experience.

A positive context is essentially an act of acceptance or appreciation and will therefore bring some form of peace or pleasure, while a negative context is an act of denial or judgement and will therefore bring some form of pain or fear.

However subtle the experience may be, making judgements is painful to us. When we judge something to be wrong or bad or threatening, we will put up a resistance to it, part of us will become tense.

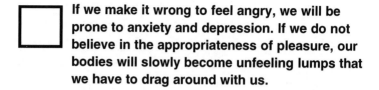 If we make it wrong to feel angry, we will be prone to anxiety and depression. If we do not believe in the appropriateness of pleasure, our bodies will slowly become unfeeling lumps that we have to drag around with us.

What we do with our minds is up to us, and this is what is meant by the religious idea of free will. We always have the choice to accept, or rail against, reality. The logical conclusion of the former is peace, and of the latter, insanity.

When looking for positive contexts to hold an experience in, excessive interest in *the* bottom line or *the* golden key is usually not that productive. What is more helpful is to realise that all experiences are multi-faceted. The break-up of a relationship, for instance, can never be just one person's fault. Many things are at play in any close relationship. When looked at under the microscope, any union is a complex jigsaw. In the same way, any situation requires a complex chain of events for it to manifest. Focusing too exclusively on any set of seemingly hard facts, therefore, is unwise.

The actual mechanics of resolving a conflict very often involve no more than becoming able to see the half empty glass as half full. When someone who has been oppressed by their rage suddenly perceives that feeling as the huge determination to DO something, something always gets done. But the shift in perception always precedes the transformation from deep depression to raw electricity. When rage has a clear, constructive outlet, there is very little it cannot achieve. When someone who has grieved long and hard over a loss realises that in that very same loss is a blessing, their whole reality changes. The grief turns to gratitude, and they experience a heartfelt thankfulness for all the precious moments they have received. This opening allows them to appreciate the fact that they have grown and become more as a result of having the person or thing that has now gone. The Relaxation Reflex is activated, and peace of mind re-established.

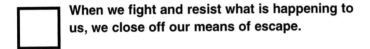

When we fight and resist what is happening to us, we close off our means of escape.

When we judge ourselves and tense against the situation, we inhibit the Relaxation Reflex, and with it creativity, imagination, flexibility, balance and insight. Our inner world will not respond to the mathematical formulae with which we dominate our external world, but it will respond to a softening of attitude. All we have to admit is there might be a better way of looking at this. Willingness is enough. Instantly our mind is opening, and with it the possibilities of the situation. We simply have to accept the experience we are having, without getting lost within it. Then, and only then, can we start working with it.

Most of the experience of life is made up of what comes to us, of what we find ourselves with. Shit happens. And the only healthy thing we can do with that shit is see it as the manure that will help us grow faster and fuller. We can't change what has already happened, but we can change the way we look at it. This is the only freedom that we truly have, but we cannot claim it until we stop running away from our feelings, and relax.

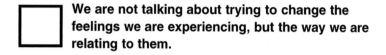

We are not talking about trying to change the feelings we are experiencing, but the way we are relating to them.

When we do that, the feelings will begin to change all on their own. If we suddenly become aware of the breathlessness of anxiety, it will not help to blithely affirm to ourselves that there is nothing to fear. It would be far more helpful to spend our time deciding whether this feeling is a sign of healthy caution or an opportunity to become a bigger, better person. It is healthy to experience anxiety when standing on the edge of a 200ft precipice, and it is natural to feel anxiety when we are about to approach the most beautiful man or woman we've ever seen.

The Relaxation Reflex is activated whenever we see the goodness in what is happening now. There have been very many people who have been helped to have a dignified death, a death without fear or despair. Some of these were assisted by a Priest, a Buddhist, a Hospice or an inner realisation, but all of them have one thing in common: they learnt, somehow, to put their death into a positive context.

Maybe they saw Jesus, maybe they got a peep into the Clear White Light they were to merge with, maybe they felt the deep gratitude of a life richly lived or maybe they just realised that death was the beautiful end to their unbearable suffering. Whatever it was, they changed the prospect of death from bad to good. And it was exactly this change in perception that brought them their peace, and their dignity.

At any moment of any day we possess the power to stop fighting with our problems and flow through them to the other side. No minute passes without giving us an opportunity to reach for the Relaxation Reflex. We are always free to see how very rich life is. Even with its ups-and-downs and nasty surprises, we can never be really sure that a mighty miracle does not wait for us around the next corner. We can never know that this insurmountable problem we are experiencing is not about to become a huge blessing. The thunder clouds might be as black as coal, and the rain may be coming down in sheets, but in twenty minutes time, who is to say that there will not be a rainbow?

A person who habitually searches for the rainbows behind their experiences is usually called an optimist, whereas a person who has the habit of finding the worst in situations is normally named a pessimist. The optimist has the ability to see painful or challenging experiences against the backdrop of a good life, while a pessimist tends to see good and bad experiences alike against the backdrop of a painful or disappointing life. As H L Menken said: "A pessimist is a man who, when he smells flowers, looks around for the coffin". This is not to put pessimism into a negative context. Some people receive an amazing amount of neglect and abuse when they are growing up. Cynicism is not a pleasurable activity, and in every case the attitude reflects the pain and disappointment that exists a little deeper.

When perception is in harmony with the heart, it has only two modes of operation: compassion and gratitude.

The first, **compassion**, is brought into play wherever there are experiences that we would have formerly called painful or challenging. We acquire the kind understanding of our own plight, we cease to hit ourselves over the head with a ruler. We put ourselves in the other person's shoes, making sure that we actually feel the hole in their sole that is letting the water in, as well as the tight cramping of their toes. In this way, our aggression becomes cooperative and creative.

The second mode of perception is **appreciation, thankfulness**, the acknowledgement that we have so much to be grateful for. And the warm, contented feeling this can bring to both belly and heart.

The heart can become powerfully united with perception when we pursue our heart's desire. This tends to colour our thinking for the better. This is the time when things begin to make sense, and we have all sorts of names for it. We may call it holding hands and making plans, building a compelling future, going for a goal, a vision quest or making a dream come true, but it is always actively going after something that we REALLY want.

There comes a time in everybody's life when they have the magnificent glimpse - a peep into a heavenly existence here on Earth. It may be a person with whom they fall in love, it might be the prospect of financial and creative satisfaction or it might be a more spiritual aspiration, but when it is fully seen, if only for a moment, it seems to make the whole of our life sparkle. It acts on our whole being like a healing balm, and makes us want it, oh so much. This inspiration, this heart's desire, this fabulous future galvanises our energy, and we begin firing on all cylinders. The past is forgiven, for it no longer matters now. We are on our way to a pre-ordained ideal state. We are high on promise, and nothing can stop us. Everything makes sense now. We know what we're here for.

Moving forward

There are many ways that people form a dream or a vision, a goal or a love object. Some dreams have been within us since childhood just waiting for the right set of circumstances to jump into. Every so often, divine inspiration just hits us out of the blue. And sometimes we get organised and set ourselves short-term, medium-term and long-term goals. Occasionally we meet someone who takes the lid off our true feelings like a can-opener. Whether we're a dreamer, a visionary, a goal-oriented achiever or a romantic, we are all drawn out of ourselves by what beckons to us from beyond. We are all attracted to something bigger and better than what we have now. And it is this pull, this reaching out, this expansion, this forward movement, that we are interested in now, rather than the objective itself.

Life is a series of ups and downs, expansions and contractions, reaching outs and pulling backs. Spring always follows Winter, and the sun always comes out after the rain. *Like the single-celled amoeba, we are constantly expanding outward to reach for our sustenance and then contracting back in to digest it*. This is how all living things grow. The tree reaches full expansion in the Summer, and then contracts during the Winter. This slow but definite pulsation makes it grow bigger each year. The same pulsative principle also occurs in human endeavour. We see something we love, something we want, and then we begin moving toward it with body, mind and soul.

This expansion is experienced as pleasurable, and the more we reach the more pleasure we have. But it never seems very long before a problem or a challenge raises its ugly head. This is the point of contraction. And also the way of life. We have expanded as much as we can for the time being. Now we are moving in again to deal with what has come up.

If we can relax at this time and ride the contraction inward, we will not only remain in tune with the movement of life but also we are far more likely to find a creative solution. In fact, this contraction is the beginning of creativity. This is the time to turn our intention inward, to draw on our inner strength and creative resources. It should not be thought of as a defeat, but a retreat. A time to withdraw and regroup, to pull back and rethink before the next movement outward.

If we can remember that there will come a contraction when we are expanding, and not forget that there follows an expansion when we are contracting, it will help us stay balanced and flexible amid the craziness of the world. This simply entails not getting cocky when we are on an expansion, and not getting sucked in when we are on a contraction.

It is remembering the ups when we are down, and keeping in mind the downs when we are on an up.

This is what is meant by the popular phrase, "being centred".

Since everything that is alive expands and contracts all the time, it should not be difficult to see that this is how we succeed and move forward. Things rarely run in one smooth line from conception to completion. There are always unexpected forks in the road, potholes, dangerous looking bends and the odd crazy driver coming at us in the middle of the road.

The most important factor in the realisation of our desires is the power of intention. The functional unity of the picture in our heads and the feeling in our hearts is more important than a detailed plan of how to get it. Ability flows out of desire, and so it is crucial that we know the desire is right before we spend time on the details. If we are to hold on to this dream with enthusiasm but without tension, and not let go of it come wind, rain or shine, it must be something that we can feel in our hearts.

This dream, this goal, this thought-form that will spearhead our energy must be worthy of us, and it must stretch us without stressing us. Ideally, we should be at peace with our present circumstances as well as knowing exactly what we are moving toward. If we are okay with what we've got now, the dream will not degenerate into an escape route, and therefore will not ultimately work against us. If we can live with our lives as they are now, it is easier to nourish our dream with loving attention, without loading other investments and agendas onto it. It is natural and healthy to have a heart's desire, and the less we wrestle with it the easier it can find its own way to fruition. The seed of our future possibilities does not require pushing and struggling, it simply needs the space and nourishment to grow in strength.

A dream that is believed in, and pursued with sincerity but without seriousness, *is* the art of not letting the bastards grind us down. It becomes like a life-jacket when we get sold down the river, and like a parachute when we take a fall. Holding on to our intention, or experiencing commitment from the heart, allows us to flex with life. Our sights are set, we know what we are aiming for, and so when the cross-currents come, as they are certain to do, we can flow with them. Furthermore, if we have a daily practice which helps us relax and which we can see is bringing us slow but definite results, it will make us even more buoyant when the sea gets choppy.

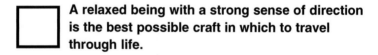

A relaxed being with a strong sense of direction is the best possible craft in which to travel through life.

We need to be centred in ourselves and focused on where we're going to be able to keep moving forward amidst all the ebbs and flows, the cross-currents and rip-tides, the ups and downs, the highs and lows, the laughter and tears, the joy and pain, the expansions and contractions.

Imagine yourself standing in the middle of a large

field. This field is covered in virgin white snow, which is glistening in the morning sunshine. Now pick a corner of the field to walk to, then close your eyes and begin walking toward it. (Give yourself a few moments to really imagine yourself doing this). Then open your eyes and look back at the tracks you've made. There is no way that you would see a straight line going in the direction you intended. Some people would have walked around in big circles and others would have gone in completely the wrong direction. Life is a bit like this, and it readily explains why so many people complain of never getting anywhere or of going round in circles. Without an aim, how can the arrow ever hit its mark? Without a destination, how can we ever get there?

When we have an inner vision that burns in our breast, we begin to see everything as a means to our end. When we can see and feel a compelling future, everything tends to get behind it. Let's take a man of God and a woman novelist as examples.

A man of God will see, or try to see, his Master's hand at work wherever he looks. When he encounters a cross-current, he will endeavour to make sense of it from this perspective.

In the same way, a novelist might see all her problems and challenges as food for thought and as material for her forthcoming novel.

The novelist may be less holy than the man of God, and the man of God may be having less fun than the novelist, but they are applying the same principle, the same creative power of intention. It is the faculty of vision that provides us with the ability to ride life in the direction it is going, all the while trusting that it will take us to that which we really want. This keeps our minds open and flexible.

It could easily be argued that to fulfil our heart's desires is the reason that we are alive, because these directional urges are not only unified with the deepest part of us but also tailor made for our personalities. The true goal of each person is the attainment of a perfect happiness, and it is quite obvious that different things make different people happy. We might just have a very practical goal to achieve health and happiness through our daily practice. We may be able to see ourselves sitting like a rock in a full lotus posture, humming with vitality and peacefulness. Or we may imagine ourselves as being able to get into a yogic position at 49 that we couldn't have done at 19. Perhaps we can see a deep, deep appreciation in our old age, perhaps we get a glimpse of us reaching the pinnacle of our profession or perhaps we can envision ourselves falling in love and actually managing to stay there.

Whatever we can see that makes us feel good, is doing us good.

Every time we see something good and wholesome in our future it gives us another good reason for being alive. The more good reasons we have for being here the more zest we will possess.

Aliveness, vitality and longevity are all very healthy

things to contemplate. Harmony, peace and abundance are ideas that have an expansive and life-giving quality. They literally nourish our mind. Cultivating the ability to reach deeper and deeper levels of relaxation really does remove the tensions that inhibit the miracle of life from flowing through us. We cannot always choose or change our circumstances, but we can always indulge in these activities. We can choose to be committed to our own well-being, and back this up with regular daily practice. We can decide to look at the quality of our thoughts and the effectiveness of the way we relate to the world, on an on-going, life-long basis. And we can reap the untold, unimaginable benefits that come from learning to hold our intention to do so.

The daily practice of some form of relaxation, taking moments here and there to daydream about our heart's desire and actively looking for the best in life are three simplicities that protect us against the ocean of contradictory information that we have to swim through on a daily basis. These three things we can, and should, control. As we develop our ability with the Relaxation Reflex and learn to see through our assumptions and preconceptions to the opportunities that are just sitting there waiting for us, we may be very pleasantly surprised.

Synchronicity

This kind of thinking tends to generate coincidences, chance encounters, lucky breaks and happy mistakes. Not because it is magical, but because we come down from our ivory tower and begin to interact with the big wide world of infinite possibilities. We begin to use more of perception's potentialities, and so we start noticing that there is more to this or that situation than meets the eye. The nuances, undertones and connections become more evident. We begin to notice unusual events, happenings that seem out of place to our routine reaction to the environment. And these episodes often amaze us.

Synchronicity is the popular expression for this type of thing, and is used to describe the experience of becoming conscious of the relationship, or connection, between events. You're thinking about someone, and just then they phone. You drive through three sets of traffic lights just as they're turning green, and it makes you feel like everything's going your way. You keep meeting people that have the same problem as you. These are the signs that you're back on the main road of your life. And as they increase and become normal and natural to you, you will be coming out of the separate cell of your mind into the unity of Life. You will realise just how tense and enclosed your perception had become.

Whether we realise it or not, synchronicity is what we all seek. It is seldom absent from any kind of success, miracle or happy event. For no matter how much effort and skill we have invested in a project, it is that final dropping into place that gives us the joy. We can go to a hundred night-clubs and dating agencies, but when we meet that Special One, it clicks effortlessly into place. Suddenly there is magic in the air, and it seems like this is pre-ordained. We can work diligently for years in our career, but when the Big One comes, nine times out of ten it is simply because we were in the right place at the right time. Even though we have done all the groundwork and made all the right noises it still seems like it just drops into our lap.

In the Natural World, all things are synchronistic. The rhythm of the tides, the cycles of the moon and sun, the seasons of growth and withdrawal, all work together in harmonious unison. What if we could learn to manifest this kind of harmony in our day-to-day experiences? What if the Relaxation Reflex caused a Parasympathetic reaction in our affairs, the events in our lives, as well as the internal restoration of harmony and happiness? What if relaxing those physical tensions helped raise the portcullis of perception, so that we could see more clearly into the outside world and notice that the enemy has gone?

What if the universe functioned on Parasympathetic principles, and the reason we keep bumping into it is because we are out of tune with our own?

Part four in a nutshell

- We generally do not choose the content of an experience, but we can exercise choice over the context we place it in.

- The way we see or interpret an experience dictates our emotional response.

- The Relaxation Reflex is activated whenever we see the goodness in what is happening now.

- A relaxed being with a strong sense of direction is the best possible craft in which to travel through life.

- An open mind tends to generate synchronicity.

Part Five

THE REFLEX
IN RELATIONSHIPS

The reflex in relationships

In a world where rape and pillage still go on, where people are still routinely tortured for their beliefs, where genocide is committed with alarming regularity, where starvation claims the lives of thousands of people every week, where nations are homeless, where more marriages break down than succeed, relationships are not always easy to conduct.

The majority of the people in the East are motivated by need, while the majority in the West are propelled by greed. North America is dominated by affluence, while South America is oppressed by poverty. Communism and capitalism, blacks and whites, the iron curtain and the bamboo curtain - there is always some conflict or another going on. Christianity, Islam, Hinduism, Judaism - there is always something to fight about. Borders, territories, states, cities, islands, continents, empires - there is always something to disagree about. The whole world is completely stressed-out, and maybe the hole in the ozone and natural disasters are stress-related symptoms of the planet.

Closer to home, how many families do you know that are not in some way dysfunctional? How many of your friends really enjoy their job? How many of your acquaintances radiate vibrant health? How many of your relationships run their course in a happy and harmonious manner?

Nowhere is stress more prevalent than in human relationships. Two people come together with different feelings, different backgrounds and different agendas. Some find a sweet dream, many a nightmare. Feelings can change quite suddenly in the course of any relationship. Business partnerships fail as readily as marriages do. There is no guarantee that the other person is going to feel the same way as they do now, further on down the road.

Yet it seems that people do not come together by accident. Synchronicity normally makes its presence felt in any fortuitous meeting. We can be introduced to hundreds of people and only really hit it off with one of them. Occasionally someone comes along who we can relate to, who activates our Relaxation Reflex, and then we form some kind of relationship with them. But why does this happen so infrequently? Is it that we are so unusual, so different, that out of all the people we run into we only find a very few who are destined to become close? Or is it that our defences are so impenetrable that only the exceptional person makes it through and sees who we are? Could it be that our tension and our attitude toward other people precludes the easy forming of friendships?

As we regularly exercise our Relaxation Reflex, it is inevitable that we will become less defensive. As we increase our ability to feel an inner well-being, we will naturally have more goodwill to extend to our fellow man. As we learn to see our shortcomings and limitations in a new light, so it will become progressively easier to give others that very same benefit of the doubt. And as we begin to inhabit our bodies more fully, to live more in harmony with them, we will be able to see more clearly what is going on with the other person. We will develop the ability to perceive the underlying pain and tension, and respond to it more effectively. Slowly it will become obvious that only someone with anxiety will be aggressive, only someone who does not feel good enough will be pushy and only someone who is unaware of their own body and feelings will barge other people out of the way.

Our relationship to our feelings never fails to have a bearing on how we are with other people. The way we relate to, or see, ourselves always has a knock-on effect. A man whose shoulders droop, whose head hangs and whose feet shuffle will not illicit great respect from passers-by. His opinion of himself is likely to be reflected in the attitude of other people. A woman who continually sacrifices her needs for that of her husband and children is more likely to get taken advantage of than receive a sainthood. If someone gives continually without giving to themselves, it is compulsion not generosity.

People notice how we hold ourselves. We are not as hidden as we imagine. ***Our bodies do not lie***, and people in general do not miss the truth they portray. The over-achiever with his puffed-up chest and his giant stride is spotted by the average person a mile away. They know exactly what he will be like when they come face to face with him. In the same way, the humble gait of a Buddhist monk tells us instantly not to expect trouble. The seductive sway of a seventeen-year old nymph, the swagger of a jack-the-lad, the gorilla-like movements of someone who lives in the gym, this information is assimilated by us in the blinking of an eye. Very, very often we know what people are like before they even open their mouths. We can tell the difference between vulnerability and aggression, depression and happiness from a single glance. We can feel the discomfort when someone is pretending not to be angry or when someone is trying to be positive when they are in fact feeling very negative. They may be fooling themselves, but they are not fooling us. Minds can deceive each other and themselves, but bodies cannot lie. The furrowed brow belies the confident attitude and the angry tone of voice betrays the reasonable words.

Human beings are more alike than they are different

Like the moon, we all have a light side as well as a dark side. We have parts of ourselves that we like and that we try to show to people, and we all have parts that we do not like and try to hide from others. We tend to be a little frightened of our dark sides, our personal demons, our skeletons in the cupboard. Bitterness and resentment, for example, are rarely embraced and shown off to the world. Debilitating disappointment is seldom expressed fully; instead we usually put a brave face on it. We tense our facial and bodily muscles, and pull ourselves together. We get a grip. In this respect, and in many others, we share the same reality. We may have different slants on it, different ways of labelling it and packing it away, but we are having more common experiences than we are having unique ones. Nobody enjoys being talked down to. No one gets off on being patronised, shouted out, demanded of, manipulated. People are not stupid. They know if you think that they are beneath you, they can feel it if you disapprove of them. Given this rather obvious information, it is surprising that the general public do not seem to see the wisdom of the Golden Rule:

Do unto others as you would have them do unto you.

The Golden Rule merely requires that we give to others the respect that we would like to get from them. Not what we *expect* to get from them, but what we would *like* to get from them. Quite simply, it is anti-cynical behaviour. And as such, it is a practice that promotes peace: the opposite of war, conflict and stress. It is a rule that forces us to try to make the world a better place. It is the wise counsel that impels us to lower our shields and lay down our weapons.

Seeing and treating others as equals can be extremely beneficial in terms of keeping the Relaxation Reflex flexing. If we have a habit of feeling above certain types, it is as certain as night following day that we will feel below other types. We can't have feelings of superiority without feelings of inferiority lurking around the next corner, since they are the two sides of one coin. People can have all sorts of gifts, but these gifts do not make them fundamentally different from other people. We are not talking about positions within society's hierarchy here, it is a human rights issue. It is the de-stressing belief that we are all in this together. This kind of thinking gives us permission to relax, because we no longer need to pour

our energy into being puffed-up and taut, nor withdrawn and resigned. We can be a unique individual, just like everyone else. It is a state of mind that allows us to be ourselves, and allows everyone else to be themselves.

Noticing that other people have feelings can only help us become more comfortable with our own. When we stop seeing our feelings as unwanted guests, we begin to see them as a sign of our humanity. It is then that they begin to work for us, instead of against us. The same is true for other people. If you really respect another person's feelings, it will not take them very long to trust you. If you keep taking another person's feelings into consideration, they will notice.

Obviously, there are people around who are so heavily armoured, so intent on winning their battle, that applying the Golden Rule to them can become a recipe for disaster. In your thoughtfulness, they'll see a doormat to wipe their shoes on, and in your kindness they'll see an easy touch. But it doesn't have to be like this. We can apply a helpful philosophy to life without forgetting our common sense. It is a rule of thumb, to be practiced as much as is reasonably possible. Thankfully, selfish, hardened people are in the minority. It is unfortunate that they feel the need to try and give the pain they feel to the world, because it can only bring them an ever increasing loneliness.

Nobody enjoys feeling lonely, unloved and disrespected. It usually drives people crazy and makes them do all sorts of desperate and destructive things. And the more these people are starved of love and approval, the more warped and twisted their thinking becomes.

Deep down though, everybody wants love and approval. They may have different names and interpretations for this most basic human commodity, but that's what they're really after. Success, wealth, prestige and fame all glitter because they are lit with the light of love and approval.

Everyone has good parts and bad parts

It is up to us which we focus upon. We can appreciate the loving licks a lioness might give to its cubs without forgetting that it would rip us to shreds if we got too close. To actively look for the best in people does not mean that we have to become naive. It is a case of neither denying nor dwelling on the dark side of people. We can notice that someone is apt to be problematic in one area, and then choose to overlook that shortcoming and see the goodness underneath or beyond it. No one is without some good points, it just depends whether we can be bothered to look for them. And if we can't be bothered, it just means that we're going to stay in the dog-eat-dog mentality, and feel the physical and emotional discomfort that are the lot of this particular attitude.

To see people only as predators will put us on guard. We simply cannot apply the Relaxation Reflex if we are expecting to be attacked. We cannot move along the road of stress-management if we think people will take advantage of us the moment we let down our defences. If we are going to relax some of the tensions in our bodies, we have to let go of some of the attacking we do in our mind's eye. This attacking occurs on two levels: toward the other person, and from the other person. The former is relatively obvious and has already been discussed, but the latter is more subtle and insidious.

It often happens that when a person is feeling fragile or vulnerable, they will see in someone else's thoughts or actions more threat or maliciousness than are actually there. "He did that on purpose", "she's trying to wind me up", "they're out to get me" are useful examples. This type of thinking is known as "projection", and is used by people to avoid taking responsibility for what they are feeling. If a group of people are out to get us, then our sense of vulnerability is their fault - we don't have to own it, or do anything about it. This kind of blame, or projection of responsibility, is as subtle and pervasive as stress itself, and requires constant vigilance until it is seen and mastered. Remember that we have to perceive threat *before* we go into a defensive mode. Don't wait till Christmas to contemplate the idea that good will to all men brings peace on earth.

The next person who knocks on the door or rings on the telephone is the one to test this philosophy on. Superior or inferior, look for the good in them, and then comment on it. You may well be amazed at how much more relaxed it makes *you* feel. Avoid the laziness of flattery, and keep looking until you find something you genuinely like and can be honest about to this person. Maybe you like his tie or her bracelet, or maybe you see a sparkle in the eye or hear a laughter in the voice. Express it, validate it, confirm it for them. It may well open a conversational door, but even if it doesn't, nine times out of ten it will make you feel happier and more confident with people.

The way we feel about other people and the way we feel about ourselves is usually not that different. People who like themselves invariably like others, and people with low self-esteem generally do not have very satisfying relationships. What we see looking back at us when we're brushing our teeth in the morning is often the way we're going to see people during the day. There, in that reflective plate of glass, is the truth about our relationships with other people. If we notice the pimples, the crooked teeth, the pasty skin, then that is the kind of thing that will be informing our perception of others.

Defining boundaries

Another area where our attitude and awareness of ourselves is mirrored in our relationships is what modern psychotherapy calls "boundaries". It is a term used to define the point which we cannot or will not go beyond. It is an expression of personal tolerance or preference, and describes much more than just the space around us. One person's alcoholic boundary might be one glass of sherry, while another's might be eleven pints of lager. We have boundaries in time-keeping and in the way we conduct relationships, and when these boundaries are crossed, differing reactions occur. If someone is 25 minutes late for an appointment with you, you're not going to be half as mad as you would be if your marriage partner slept with someone else. Like people, boundaries come in all shapes and sizes. They can be strong or weak, flexible or rigid. And they can be abused by ourselves or by others.

Learning about our boundaries can help us no end in understanding other people's boundaries. When we respect the lines we draw for ourselves, the places where we will not go beyond, it becomes easier to extend the same respect to other people. Boundaries are not barbed wire fences. They are safety margins that define our comfort zones. When we cross these margins, or other people do, we experience anything from mild irritation to extreme rage, from dull aches to searing pain. They represent our current limitations, and to disrespect them is to deny reality.

Barbara Brennan, in her book, *Hands of Light*, describes the human energy field as extending out to four feet from the body. Now, if you imagine this phenomenon happening to you as you get pleasantly lost in your novel on the train, and then some oaf in pin-stripes plonks his drunken body down next to you, you're going to feel that reverberate through your entire being. On a feeling level, this guy has just completely abused your boundaries (even if, in terms of society's boundaries, he has every right to land next to you). Whilst this may seem like an unavoidable incident, it can be of immense value to understand why we react like we do. Being aware of our boundaries allows us to react to the situation without intrinsically hating the other person. And this allows us to get back to the Relaxation Reflex with greater speed and efficiency.

People are often unaware of their own as well as other people's boundaries. Many people don't really know where they stop and the other person begins. They merge with their partners and form dependant relationships that smother and stifle originality and creativity. These people frequently over step the mark, gatecrash or go over the top. Their inherent anxiety makes them push or cling, but rarely just be who they are. It is helpful to remember, however, that if this kind of person had violent parents or was hated as a baby, they may have had their Sympathetic Nervous Systems jammed on since that time. They may never have felt the warm, reassuring, independent waves of well-being that run through a balanced and healthy nervous system. (Unfortunately, those who experienced insecure infancies have to work a lot harder to "find themselves" than someone who got the love they needed. Fortunately, abused or emotionally starved children often grow up gifted, and with not a little grit).

There are others who are wilfully unaware of boundaries. Maybe the boundaries they were given as children were brutally harsh and now their delayed reaction is to show as much disrespect as they can to boundaries wherever they happen to see them. Still others know where their boundaries are but rigidly adhere to them, without gaining the necessary flexibility to ride over the rough terrain of life. Or else their boundaries may be too flexible, in which case they end up feeling overwhelmed all the time or taken advantage of.

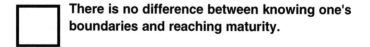

There is no difference between knowing one's boundaries and reaching maturity.

Each boundary we learn about as we are growing up serves to make us safer and wiser. Take the cliche of the child playing with fire as an example. He soon learns that there is a boundary between him and the fire. Slowly we

114

come to understand what we can and cannot do, what we like and what we dislike, what we can comfortably tolerate and what gives us pain. These are the boundaries that define who we are at present. And even the boundaries that are floppy or steel-like create the chinks in our character that make us human and unique. The more we perceive our limitations in a healthy way, the more our boundaries will work for us and the easier we will find it to turn on the Relaxation Reflex.

Boundaries are really just the places where our pleasure and well-being stops. To deny them, to disrespect them, to be unaware of them simply leads to more tension and pain.

Any relationship requires some negotiation of boundaries. And the more we are aware of our boundaries, the easier it will be to draw them in or expand them at will. We can't have an intimate relationship unless we are prepared to open up and let the other person in. Nor can we function well within the rat race unless we can draw our boundaries in. Ideally, they should be both flexible and strong, and the more we relax and tune into our feelings the more naturally this will occur.

It is all a matter of finding our own rhythm, our own vibration, our own pace. We have to experiment and find what works for us. If we take no notice of our feelings, we lose balance and flexibility. If we take too much notice of our feelings, we also lose balance and flexibility. It is very similar to holding a bird in the hand. Hold it too tightly and it'll suffocate; hold it too lightly and it'll fly away. This is not only true for our relationship with ourselves and our bodies but also for relationships in general.

Not many people like being smothered, and not many like feeling that they don't matter either. Staying tuned-in to what's happening on the inside of us as well as the outside of us, and staying flexible in mind and body are really the same thing. One feeds the other. The divide between us and other people is not as great as many of us imagine. We tend to feel separate from others *because* we feel separate from ourselves.

As we make a commitment to our own well-being, we will naturally feel more commitment to the well-being of others and the world. As we come to terms with our own compartments of selfishness, childishness or defensiveness, it will become less of a problem when we see the same thing in other people. And as we slowly find healthy ways to relate to our so-called negative feelings, we will find it increasingly easy to understand the great difficulty most people have in expressing these emotions. We will slowly reach a compassionate understanding of why people have to be indirect, underhanded and sometimes thoroughly unpleasant. Their behaviour is an expression of the relationship they are having with themselves. No one can be nasty to others for very long without a psychic boomerang coming back in their face. Yes, they can keep on tensing, keep hardening their exterior, keep turning up the aggression, but there is no way that this line of action can make them feel good inside.

Take Hitler for example. He may have had a hardened exterior while he was trying to exterminate a whole race, but he suffered from a whole litany of physical complaints, chief among which was the most atrocious indigestion. It seems that his gut feeling was rather different from his utopian vision!

Most people do not mean to be thoughtless and selfish, they are just lost in their own little stressed-out world. They are just fulfilling what they consider to be their needs. Their Sympathetic Nervous System is switched on and they don't know how to switch it off. Consequently, life for them is a survival issue. They look at life and the world and secretly wonder whether they're going to make it through. The anxiety gnaws away at their stomachs, and their inner demons continue to haunt them. They do not have the room within themselves to consider other people, and this is one of the reasons why their anxiety and paranoia are self-perpetuating. Unfortunately, there is not much we can do for them, except to furnish them with an example of someone who has changed his or her mind, one who has chosen a different mode of being. The only way to change the world is to change the way we see it and relate to it. And the only way to improve our relationships is to improve our relationship to ourselves, by practicing the Relaxation Reflex.

Having poor relations with other people is stressful. If we feel uncomfortable with someone it puts us on edge. If we harbour a grievance toward someone, it makes us tense. The opposite is just as true. If we are on good terms with everyone, it makes us relax and feel safe. When we are comfortable with other people, it becomes an enriching and rewarding experience to spend time with them. When we choose to overlook a mistake, to let it ride, it maintains our well-being and peace of mind. When we try and give people a bit of lift, a helping hand, it is also our sense of well-being that we are giving a lift to. We are keeping ourselves sweet by keeping other people sweet. After all, life is a reciprocal process.

Humanity is far from perfect, and yet it holds within it the seed of perfection. If it could learn to conquer stress like it has conquered so many other things, the human species would take a giant evolutionary step forward. The vast reserves of life and money that are poured into wars could be used in a creative direction. All the scientists that devise ingenious ways to kill people could turn their attention to gadgets that produced pleasure and satisfaction. All the great medical minds could be freed up to spend more time improving health and longevity. And all those broken dreams could be resurrected and brought to life.

Being realistic and admitting that the way it is, is the way it is, does not mean that we have to forget the infinite possibilities that lie before us. Just because we live in a crazy world does not mean that we will not see giant strides toward a happier world in this lifetime. We can accept things the way they are without losing our faith in human nature.

As Oscar Wilde said,

> *"We are all in the gutter, but some of us*
> *are looking at the stars"*

Part five in a nutshell

- The way we feel about ourselves and the way we feel about others is usually not that different.

- Being friendly and understanding activates the Relaxation Reflex and makes us feel better about ourselves.

- Boundaries represent our current limitations, and to disrespect them is to deny reality.

- The more we perceive our limitations in a healthy way, the more our boundaries will work for us and the easier relaxation will become.

Conclusion

When the misty haze of religious and philosophical thought has cleared, we see that Heaven is ruled by love, and Hell is dominated by fear. It then begins to dawn on us that this is also an accurate description of the two possible habitual modes of man's Autonomic Nervous System.

When we have clambered through the complexities that psychology and physiology have to offer, we realise that it is fear which stimulates the Sympathetic and love which activates the Parasympathetic. Whenever, wherever and however love is actually felt, it is always a warm, expansive and pleasurable feeling. The loss or rejection of love very often brings fear and pain, but love itself is always a pleasure. It may have the force of sexual desire behind it, it may take on a more parental and benevolent appearance, it may express itself through a heart that is devoted to serving one's fellow man, it may erupt spontaneously without a particular focus, or it may maintain a low key presence in the form of well-being, but it is always a pleasure to experience.

Because of events in the past, many people associate pain with this wonderful feeling and in so doing have given rise to the popular term, "pleasure anxiety". It is a deeply ironic fact that underneath their anxiety and within their tension, lies the independent well-being that can cure them of their malady. This natural love that waits, dormant in the depths, can be *rejected* by another but only *extinguished* by oneself.

There are always fears to be faced in any self-resurrection, but none that may not be overcome with love. As we learn to worry less and relax more, we become stronger in the force of love, the power of feeling good. We become more tuned into the *connectedness* of things, the natural order. Our sixth sense becomes more acute. We become better able to take a knock here and a bruise there. The knocks no longer steal our balance because we have been practicing our poise, and the bruises don't hurt so much because we have more pleasure inside of us. We are getting used to the presence of pleasure in our mind and body. Love is beginning to feel natural to us.

The Relaxation Reflex comes into play when we treat our minds and bodies with love. Our relationships begin to work when we apply a little love to a heated situation. And our problems, our conflicts, our tensions begin to loosen the moment we look at ourselves with kind and understanding eyes.

It may take a little while for the solution, resolution or relaxation to come, but the second we extend some love to ourselves, things lighten a little. As we continue giving ourselves what we need, things lighten a lot.

Health is harmony: the free and unified flow of fluids and feelings through our bodies.

When we are not feeling threatened or being defensive, we experience this feeling of harmony as love. In exactly the same way as the Parasympathetic, love makes its presence known once we begin to feel safe, once we have let go of the fear, once we are moving away from our Sympathetic reaction. This feeling of pleasure inside us, when it comes, is the answer to the question of who am I? Once we can feel love inside of us, we no longer feel separate and lost. And who would not begin to feel lost and separate if they were unable to feel anything good inside themselves?

Life without an inner sense of well-being does indeed seem a futile and disorienting process.

The claiming and owning of our birthright to unconditional well-being rests on our ability to practice a quiet and natural pleasure as regularly as possible until we are able to relax and surrender to the symphony of sensations we have the potential to feel. We cannot be held back by other people in this quest to be all we can be, but we can apply the brakes of apathy and lack of commitment.

The possibilities of pleasure are unlimited. We are limited only by our fear and tension. Fear can be faced and dispelled, and tension can be relaxed. These are skills that we can learn, no matter how far down the pit we may be at present. The reward, the grail, the magical ability that is won by maintaining a gentle discipline is greater and deeper well-being, pleasure and happiness. In short, love; that cohesive force that we feel in our hearts and flesh when we experience harmony, happiness and good fortune, or when we respond to bad fortune with compassion.

The Relaxation Reflex is gentle, it is flowing, it is pleasurable, it is expansive, it is rich, it is miraculous.

In a nutshell, the Relaxation Reflex is Love.

Other related titles from Management Books 2000

📖 *Change Your Thinking, Change Your Life*
Phil Underwood

📖 *The Frog Snogger's Guide*
Susan Lancaster and Sean Orford

📖 *Maximise Your Potential*
Ian Seymour

📖 *What Colour is Your Knicker Elastic?*
Sean Orford

📖 *Winners Win and Losers Lose*
Nick Thornely and Dan Lees

Index